T0149254

Kene D. Ewulu, Ed.D.

CHRIST-LED REBOUND SERIES

INACTIVITY

WESTBOW
P R E S S®
A DIVISION OF THOMAS NELSON
& ZONDERVAN

WestBow Press books may be ordered through booksellers or by contacting:

WestBow Press
A Division of Thomas Nelson & Zondervan
1663 Liberty Drive
Bloomington, IN 47403
www.westbowpress.com
1 (866) 928-1240

Because of the dynamic nature of the Internet, any web addresses or
links contained in this book may have changed since publication and may
no longer be valid. The views expressed in this work are solely those
of the author and do not necessarily reflect the views of the publisher,
and the publisher hereby disclaims any responsibility for them.

Any people depicted in stock imagery provided by Thinkstock are
models, and such images are being used for illustrative purposes only.
Certain stock imagery © Thinkstock.

ISBN: 978-1-5127-2740-1 (sc)
ISBN: 978-1-5127-2739-5 (e)

Library of Congress Control Number: 2016900962

Print information available on the last page.

WestBow Press rev. date: 01/20/2016

Contents

Author's Note

In my first book, titled *Christ-Led Rebound Principles: Sustaining Christian Deliverance and Victory*, life's issues that we struggle with were identified, scripturally backed solutions were proffered, and ways of keeping our victory were outlined.

I have, however, realized that modern Christians and non-Christians seldom read large amounts of print due to the proliferation of audio and video mediums. I also realized that readers would want smaller booklets that deal with their peculiar and respective struggles. In essence, someone struggling with the backlash of separation and divorce may not necessarily want to learn how to deal with the scourge of unemployment or depression.

The Lord has therefore led me to break up the original book into small booklets that deal with these singular struggles or *yokes*, and to delve deeper into the action steps we must embrace in order to be delivered from them and live free, victorious lives in Christ.

This first publication of the Christ-Led Rebound Series addresses *inactivity*. Read, meditate, and practice what you learn, and live right by the grace and strengthening of our Lord Jesus Christ, and the Holy Spirit of God.

May the Lord Jesus enlighten your mind and spirit as you read, and may He give you the strength and discipline to put the revelations gleaned here into action.

Blessings from the King of Kings!

Dr. Kene D. Ewulu

January 2016

The thief cometh not, but for to steal, and to kill, and to destroy: I am come that they might have life, and that they might have it more abundantly.

(John 10:10, KJV)

Dedication

This work is dedicated to my Lord
and Savior, Jesus Christ.
Who has the singular assignment of humbly walking
the earth, obediently suffering to death on the Cross,
valiantly wresting the keys of hell from the devil, and
continually interceding for everyone in Heaven
Your creation acknowledges your unmatchable
power and unquestionable love.
We love you!

Dr. Kene D. Ewulu
January 2016

Preamble

There is a popular secular adage that states that "an idle mind is the devil's workshop." It means that we are not supposed to operate within a vacuum because ungodly thoughts and actions emanate from idleness or lack of reward-focused activity. We are created to be actively involved in some sort of activity, be it fruitful or counterproductive.

Scripture also says that we have to work in order to eat (2 Thessalonians 3:10), and that whatsoever we sow, we will reap (Galatians 6:7). The person who sows the wind reaps the whirlwind (Hosea 8:7), and the person who sows good seed diligently is promised great rewards (Psalms 126:5-6).

In all respects, therefore, we have to be actively involved in producing something; the opposite results in idleness, laziness, and inactivity, which does not bode well for us. This treatise focuses on avoiding inactivity and embracing habitually good practices that promise success and fulfillment. May the Lord God bless you as you internalize the precepts presented herein.

Amen.

Defining Inactivity

The work of redemption by our Lord Jesus—and the ensuing Christian walk by believers—is a constant spiritual battle that will neither abate nor end until Christ's triumphant second coming and eventual victory over Satan.

We are expected to make gains in the ongoing spiritual warfare through the reading and exposition of God's Word to our families and the rest of humanity. When we become lethargic or inactive in this respect, we cede some ground to the Enemy, because there can never be a vacuum in the realm of the spirit; the army is either advancing or retreating!

Unfortunately, many people fall into spiritual, physical, and mental inactivity or laziness by giving themselves excuses for not exercising their God-given talents and energies. The Bible records two of these as fear of the unknown and slothfulness.

> The slothful man saith, There is a lion without, I shall be slain in the streets. (Proverbs 22:13 KJV)

> As the door turneth upon his hinges, so doth the slothful upon his bed. The slothful hideth his hand in his bosom; it grieveth him to bring it again to his mouth. The sluggard is wiser in his own conceit than seven men that can render a reason. (Proverbs 26:14–16)

An example of the danger of spiritual inactivity occurred when Eli, the high priest, allowed his sons' misdemeanors in the temple of the Lord to continue without correction.

> Now Eli was very old, and he heard all that his sons were doing to all Israel, and how they lay with the women who served at the entrance to the tent of meeting. And he said to them, Why do you do such things? For I hear of your evil dealings from all the people. No, my sons; it is no good report that I hear the people of the Lord spreading abroad. If a man sins against a man, God will mediate for him; but if a man sins against

the Lord, who can intercede for him? But they would not listen to the voice of their father; for it was the will of the Lord to slay them. (1 Samuel 2:22–25 RSV)

It is noteworthy that Eli did warn his children about the potential consequences of their morally bankrupt behavior: fornication and greed. However, God was angry with Eli because he did not use his position as high priest and father to stop the abominable activities. Neither did he repent and ask for a chance to remedy the situation when God confirmed the impending punishment upon his house:

So Samuel told him everything and hid nothing from him. And he said, It is the Lord; let him do what seems good to him. (1 Samuel 3:18 RSV)

Although it may not always seem so, God created man and imbued him with courage, strength of character, and leadership ability. Leadership in this context is the capacity and willingness to blaze a new trail, to step out into unfamiliar territory, and to lead our families on the straight-and-narrow path of righteousness, regardless

3

of how unfashionable it may seem in our world of today. Our spouses, children, peers, and society as a whole will prosper in all they do if we as men and leaders in our homes take a stand to walk according to God's instructions. If we profess to love them, then we must take that stand now. Our loved ones and we will be blessed and exalted when we walk in the righteousness of God:

> Righteousness exalteth a nation: but sin is a reproach to any people. (Proverbs 14:34 KJV)

We need to arise from our slumber and get active. The Lord reminds us that any man who refuses to work will not be able to feed himself and that laziness is a prelude to poverty in body and in spirit.

> How long wilt thou sleep, O sluggard? when wilt thou arise out of thy sleep? Yet a little sleep, a little slumber, a little folding of the hands to sleep: So shall thy poverty come as one that travelleth, and thy want as an armed man. (Proverbs 6:9–11 KJV)

The time to act is *now*!

When studying, praying, and acting on the Word of God takes a back seat in a man's life, it is a dangerous sign that spiritual inactivity has set in. Furthermore, because we have acted as spiritual leaders in our homes and places of endeavor in times past, the Devil has identified us as potential threats to his kingdom. Satan will therefore do all that he can in order to subjugate and oppress us if our activity in the things of the Lord diminish to the level where God's umbrella of protection is no longer available for us.

Inactivity begins in the spiritual realm and spills over into the physical, social, and emotional aspects of our lives.

- *Inactivity* can be defined as "lethargy" or "reluctance" in reading the Word of God and in praying or in being committed and involved with the local church and their programs.
- *Inactivity* can be described as laziness or reluctance to exert our full energies toward daily tasks.

- In the physical world you can hold your ground even if you are not advancing. But in the spiritual world, there is no vacuum—you are either advancing or retreating, and there is no middle ground.

- Being inactive or ignorant puts you under the Devil's rule.

- Examples of inactivity are not putting thoughts or ideas into action, not reading the Word, not praying, and not acting on the Word.

- Inactivity is a bad habit that diminishes and impoverishes us physically, emotionally, and spiritually.

Rebounding from Inactivity

For God so loved the world, that he gave his only begotten Son, that whoso- ever believeth in him should not perish, but have everlasting life. (John 3:16 KJV)

Rebounding from inactivity can be achieved by following certain established, practical steps. These steps require personal discipline and dedication, and they are outlined below:

- Read the Bible frequently and consistently.
- Designate a convenient, quiet time, preferably early in the morning, for daily study of the Bible.
- Pray for God's enlightenment before each study session, and allot a reasonable amount of time daily for this exercise.
- Always end your study sessions with a word of prayer.

- Ask God to ignite your passion for His Word and to help you remember the words you have learned throughout the day.
- Stay active in a local church; take advantage of opportunities to fellowship frequently.
- Do what you have been led by God to do; obey, be brave, and step out in faith.
- Be a person of action; back up your insights with action.
- Do not worry or be discouraged. God has promised to bless the work of your hands if you commit your ways to Him.

We will now look at these practical steps in greater detail.

1. Read the Bible frequently and consistently.

> Thy word is a lamp unto my feet, and a light unto my path. (Psalm 119:105 KJV)

Doing this diligently serves to wash us clean, purifying our thought processes and giving us power to not only resist the Devil but also to hear from God and pursue our activities with belief and vigor.

2. Designate a convenient, quiet time, preferably early in the morning, for daily study of the Bible.

> This book of the law shall not depart out of thy mouth; but thou shalt meditate therein day and night, that thou mayest observe to do according to all that is written therein: for then thou shalt make thy way prosperous, and then thou shalt have good success. (Joshua 1:8 KJV)

Forming a quiet-time habit can help bring structure to our daily study of the Bible. Waking up fifteen minutes earlier every morning to read the Word, for example, allows us take in God's instruction when our home is quiet—and when our brains are fresh from a good night's sleep.

3. Pray for God's enlightenment before and during each study session; allot a reasonable amount of time daily for this exercise.

> Study to show thyself approved unto God, a workman that needed not to be ashamed, rightly dividing the word of truth. (2 Timothy 2:15 KJV)

Asking God in prayer to teach us something specific during our upcoming study session is wise. This way, the inspired Word of God jumps out at us from the written Word; we receive a fresh revelation each time we add prayer to our study sessions.

4. Always end our study sessions with a word of prayer, asking God to keep all we learned safe in our heart and thanking Him for speaking to us through His Word.

> Continue in prayer, and watch in the same with thanksgiving. (Colossians 4:2 KJV)

> Pray without ceasing. (1 Thessalonians 5:17 KJV)

> Praying always with all prayer and supplication in the Spirit, and watching thereunto with all perseverance and supplication for all saints. (Ephesians 6:18 KJV)

Prayer is our spiritual food; it keeps us strong, sensitive to the movement of God, and full of faith to accomplish our designated tasks. Prayer lets us into God's presence to acknowledge Him as our ever-present help in every situation. It gives us the chance on a daily basis to show our gratitude to God and strengthens our desire to retain and implement all we learned.

5. **Ask God to ignite your passion for His Word and to help you remember the words you have learned throughout the day.**

> With my whole heart have I sought thee: O let me not wander from thy commandments. Thy word have I hid in mine heart, that I might not sin against thee. I will meditate in thy precepts, and have respect unto thy ways. I will delight myself in thy statutes: I will not forget thy word. (Psalm 119:10–11, 15–16 KJV)

This prayer can be said after our study time; it ensures that every prayer we said—and every revelation we received as a result of our quiet time with our heavenly

Father—stays with us. It reminds us during the day that victory is already within our grasp, and it enables us to reject the accusations of the Evil One.

6. Stay active in a local church.

> Not forsaking the assembling of ourselves together, as the manner of some is; but exhorting one another: and so much the more, as ye see the day approaching. (Hebrews 10:25 KJV)

Several opportunities abound for keeping active in Christian events during the week. We can attend Sunday services, midweek fellowships, or home groups, or utilize web casts, podcasts, and smartphone apps. The goal is to try to attend at least two congregational activities weekly; this habit keeps us immersed in God's Word during the week, strengthens us, and protects us from the Evil One.

7. Do what you have been led by God to do: obey, be brave, and step out in faith.

> Every place that the sole of your foot shall tread upon, that have I given unto you, as I said unto

Moses. Have not I commanded thee? Be strong and of a good courage; be not afraid, neither be thou dismayed: for the Lord thy God is with thee whithersoever thou goest. (Joshua 1:3, 9 KJV)

When you are a doer of the Word, you act in obedience; and God prefers obedience to everything else, rewarding it bountifully.

And Samuel said, Hath the Lord as great delight in burnt offerings and sacrifices, as in obeying the voice of the Lord? Behold, to obey is better than sacrifice, and to hearken than the fat of rams. (1 Samuel 15:22 KJV)

8. Resolve to be a person of action; back up your insights with action.

What doth it profit, my brethren, though a man say he hath faith, and have not works? Can faith save him? For as the body without the spirit is dead, so faith without works is dead also. (James 2:14, 26 KJV)

By resolving to be persons of action, we back up our insights and ideas with sustained action, as outlined by this verse:

> Seest thou a man diligent in his business? He shall stand before kings; he shall not stand before mean men. (Proverbs 22:29 KJV)

God has promised to grant us extraordinary success if we obey and diligently pursue our assigned tasks; He has promised to grant us favor before those in authority, and to shield us from those who would impede our progress.

9. Do not worry or be discouraged. God has promised to bless the work of your hands if you commit your ways to Him.

> Trust in the Lord with all thine heart; and lean not unto thine own understanding. In all thy ways acknowledge him, and he shall direct thy paths. (Proverbs 3:5–6 KJV)

A word of caution: we must not confuse inactivity with rest. We are to resist inactivity but embrace the seasons of rest that come after we have exerted ourselves spiritually and physically.

Lethargy or inactivity is encouraged by several excuses; these range from fear of failure to pride, obstinacy, lack of confidence, and sheer laziness. The scriptures warn us of laziness:

> Yet a little sleep, a little slumber, a little folding of the hands to sleep: So shall thy poverty come as one that travels; and thy want as an armed man. (Proverbs 24:33–34 KJV)

But if and when we obey and act, we will prosper in ways we cannot comprehend, and God's name will be glorified by our breakthroughs. Worrying is a sign of disbelief in God's promises, so we have to do all we can not to worry about the success of our endeavors.

God has promised; He always delivers!

Victory Through Spiritual Activity

Jesus has a response for us as we battle lethargy, inactivity, laziness, and fear of the unknown. He says:

> Come unto me, all ye that labor and are heavy laden, and I will give you rest. Take my yoke upon you, and learn of me; for I am meek and lowly in heart: and ye shall find rest unto your souls. For my yoke is easy, and my burden is light. (Matthew 11:28–30 KJV)

In order to be a doer of the Word and victorious in Jesus Christ, we must get active, arise, and place our burdens at the only place they can be taken care of: at the foot of Jesus!!

A few practical steps to retaining our victory through spiritual activity are praise and worship, integrating the buddy system in our lives, and being of service to others.

Kene D. Ewulu, Ed.D.

▪ Praise and Worship

Learning to praise and worship God with songs, whether verbally or in our minds, is a sure way to stay in His presence continually. Praise attracts God.

> But thou art holy, O thou that inhabitest the praises of Israel. (Psalms 22:3 KJV)

When God is present wherever we are, His joy pervades our whole being. Joy is the inexplicable happiness we feel, not just for what we have, but for who we are in God. Joy does not depend on our circumstances, but stems from our knowledge that God will always stand by us through our storms and our calms.

> Thou wilt shew me the path of life: in thy presence is fullness of joy; at thy right hand there are pleasures for evermore. (Psalms 16:11 KJV)

With God's joy come strength, freedom, and pleasurable things.

> The Lord is my strength and my shield; my heart trusted in him, and I am helped: therefore my

heart greatly rejoiceth; and with my song will I praise him. (Psalms 28:7 KJV)

Then he said unto them, Go your way, eat the fat, and drink the sweet, and send portions unto them for whom nothing is prepared: for this day is holy unto our Lord: neither be ye sorry; for the joy of the Lord is your strength. (Nehemiah 8:10 KJV)

Praise and worship to our heavenly Father brings down His presence, and with His presence comes joy, strength, victory, and peace.

- **The Buddy System**

This system advocates that a person rebounding from inactivity should find a mature Christian to be accountable to; this confirms the biblical principle of unity, whereby two or more unified persons can achieve so much more than if they stood alone.

Again I say unto you, That if two of you shall agree on earth as touching anything that they shall ask, it shall be done for them of my Father which is in heaven. For where two or three are

> gathered together in my name, there am I in the midst of them. (Matthew 18:19–20 KJV)

We need to find someone who shares our values concerning our peculiar situations and agrees with them. This mature Christian should ideally be a spirit-filled, committed, and resolute Christian believer who is willing to give of his time and spirituality for the benefit and growth of others. We then encourage each other during times of weakness, say prayers of agreement as needed, and celebrate our milestones, no matter how small they might be.

> Again, if two lie together, then they have heat: but how can one be warm alone? And if one prevail against him, two shall withstand him; and a threefold cord is not quickly broken. (Ecclesiastes 4:11–12 KJV)

▪ Service to Others

When we focus on being useful or helpful to others, our needs pale in comparison to theirs. When we place others' needs above ours, we love them as Christ commanded, and heap rewards for ourselves here and in the afterlife. There is also an inexplicable sense of worth that comes from making something good happen for someone else.

> I have shewed you all things, how that so laboring ye ought to support the weak, and to remember the words of the Lord Jesus, how he said, It is more blessed to give than to receive. (Acts 20:35 KJV)

The icing on the cake, however, is the universal understanding that when we engage in any activity of service to others, we are not only helping them, but we are true leaders. The oft-repeated political cliché of "elected to serve the people" stems from this truth. To lead means we have to serve, as explained by our Lord Jesus:

> But so shall it not be among you: but whosoever will be great among you, shall be your minister: And whosoever of you will be the chiefest, shall be servant of all. (Mark 10:43–44 KJV)

Epilogue

King Solomon advises us to do our work diligently and conscientiously:

> Whatsoever thy hand findeth to do, do it with thy might; for there is no work, nor device, nor knowledge, nor wisdom, in the grave, whither thou goest. (Ecclesiastes 9:10 KJV)

No job or vocation is too menial to apply a strong work ethic to. Obviously, when we perform small tasks well, promotion is along the way because superiors encourage more productive workers through more responsibilities and higher rewards. The case for putting in our best into our tasks is further strengthened by understanding that there will come a time when we are too old for productive work and its commensurate rewards. Urgency to work hard, work well, and maximize our earnings should be our watchword!

Staying active is an art we must practice in order to be successful and to lead meaningful lives. Using our days wisely means utilizing every waking hour toward accomplishing set tasks. Battling inactivity requires then that we pray, study the word of God, fellowship with others, put our ideas into action, persevere at what we do, and refuse to be discouraged. These actions require that we not look too far ahead, but take one step at a time, planning our work and then working our plan. God sees this as faith, and He will show us the way and make the journey easier:

> And I will bring the blind by a way that they knew not; I will lead them in paths that they have not known: I will make darkness light before them, and crooked things straight. These things will I do unto them, and not forsake them. (Isaiah 42:16 KJV)

Stay active, trust God for victory, and win.

Glossary

Christ-Led Rebound: The process of recovery from personal challenges, which incorporates biblical instructions, insight, encouragement, and prayers offered to God through His son, Jesus Christ. The complete dependence on the promises of Jesus Christ, that He will set us permanently and completely free when we profess His Lordship and obey foundational Christian beliefs.

Yoke: Any challenge we face that might have emanated from the spiritual. Lying, greed, envy, and sexual immorality are examples of yokes that spring from the devil. Jesus's yoke, however, is easy because He loves us, died for us, and ever lives to intercede for us in God the Father's presence. We are commanded to put on Jesus's yoke.

Inactivity: Lethargy or reluctance in reading the Word of God, in praying, or in being committed and involved with the local church and their programs. In the secular world, inactivity can be defined as laziness or reluctance to exert our full energies toward daily tasks.

Meditate: To study deeply and take enough time to think on what one studied. It is advisable to pray for clarity and understanding before meditating on the Word of God.

Redemption: Buying back a debt from someone. Release from accountability or payment; forgiveness and a new start. The Blood of Jesus was shed on the cross so all sinners (we all) are forgiven and redeemed from the clutches of the devil. Believing that Jesus died for us and accepting Him as Lord and Savior assures us of redemption and, subsequently, salvation.

Spiritual Battle: The fight between good and evil that rages on in the spiritual realm. Everything that happens to us in the physical first occurs in the spiritual. Our prayer to God is a spiritual battle; it precedes God's blessings, and that is why Jesus asked us to ask, seek, and knock so we can receive, find, and have open doors. Spiritual battles will go on until Jesus Christ's triumphant second coming.

Slothfulness: Performing our assignments haphazardly or in a sloppy manner. Going through our daily tasks with laziness of mind, spirit, and body; lack of organization and untidiness.

Leadership: Inspiring and motivating others to excellence through support, understanding, and being non-judgmental.

Love: Being charitable, empathetic, supportive, and encouraging to others. Emulating Jesus and placing others' needs ahead of ours. Sacrificially giving of our time, resources, and energy to others.

Righteousness: The desire to do what is right and acceptable before the eyes of God. This can actually translate into successfully living right before God, but God looks first at the intentions of the heart. Exhibiting and utilizing other fruits of the Spirit, such as faith, patience, self-control, gentleness, and humility, are virtues that God admires in us and which He can use as yardsticks for holy living or righteousness. Note that in order to resist the devil and be righteous, we all need God's help and enablement.

Poverty: A body, mind, or spirit that is in dire need. The need could be physical lack (money, clothes, health) or a mental lack (stable mind, joy, peace, etc.).

Enlightenment: A deeper understanding of a subject or situation; a fresh revelation or insight. This often happens when we study and meditate on something for a while.

Quiet Time: A time set aside for reading the Word of God, praying, or listening to/singing songs of praise to God.

Obedience: Following God's instructions, even when we do not understand the reasoning or logic behind them. God values obedience above so many things because we display our trust in Him when we obey Him without questioning.

Diligence: Applying steady hard work and attention to the smallest details of our tasks. We are also diligent when we refuse to quit during challenging and difficult periods.

Rest: Complete faith in God. A place in our minds where we can drop every worry or anxiety and believe without any doubt that God will intervene for our good. The place where God's peace, which surpasses all understanding, is experienced and enjoyed.

Praise: Extolling God for the things He has done for us, or in other cases, for the things we believe that He will yet do for us. God can be praised through our voices or by utilizing musical instruments.

Worship: A higher form of praise where we extol God for who He is, and not necessarily for the things He has done for us. A scenario where we just want to be in His presence, and where we are not necessarily asking Him for anything!

The Buddy System: An accountability system where we join with someone of like mind to believe in God for an expected provision, healing, protection, or insight. Leveraging the understanding that where two or more people stand together, the power of unity is released and extraordinary breakthroughs occur.

Unity: Agreeing on something together; this often leads to exceptional victories, even more so if we are in unity with God. Knowing God's will for a situation and aligning with His will depicts perfect unity.

Service: Helping others through their difficulties; supporting others and giving back to our communities.

About the Author

Kene D. Ewulu is a professor of organizational leadership and project management, an ordained pastor, and the author of the Christ-Led Rebound Series. He combines his academic pursuits with an empathetic heart for his fellow man. He is burning with the passion to enable men and women to embrace their God-given mandates as spiritual leaders and moral compasses at home, work, and in their communities.

He is the founder and vice president of the Caleb Assembly, a non-profit Christian ministry based in Columbia, South Carolina. The Caleb Assembly facilitates seminars and retreats for churches, motivates people in halfway homes, and challenges others to rebound onto righteous living through their weekly global newsletters.

Kene resides in Columbia with his wife, Ijeoma, and their three teenage children.

Contact

www.thecalebassembly.org
kdewulu@thecalebassembly.org

Other Publications

Christ-Led Rebound Principles: Sustaining Christian
Deliverance and Victory

Printed in the United States
By Bookmasters